Let's Learn American Sign Language

FAMILY

Raymie Davis

Illustrations By:
Brad Manker,
35 Corks Art Studio

PowerKiDS press.

PK Beginners

I can sign
about my family.

I use my hands.

mom

dad

sister

brother

grandma

grandpa

aunt

uncle

cousin

friend

Published in 2025 by The Rosen Publishing Group, Inc.
2544 Clinton Street, Buffalo, NY 14224

First Edition

Special thanks to Michelle Rose, M.S., American Sign Language Consultant

Book Design: Tanya Dellaccio Keeney
Illustrator: Brad Manker, 35 Corks Art Studio

Photo Credits: Cover (girl) ktaylorg/iStock.com; cover (background pattern) Olgastocker/Shutterstock.com; p. 3 Prostock-studio/Shutterstock.com; pp. 5, 7, 19 fizkes/Shutterstock.com; p. 9 altafulla/Shutterstock.com; p. 11 MIA Studio/Shutterstock.com; p. 13 New Africa/Shutterstock.com; p. 15 LightField Studios/Shutterstock.com; p. 17 Dragon Images/Shutterstock.com; p. 21 Samuel Borges Photography/Shutterstock.com; p. 23 Robert Kneschke/Shutteratock.com.

Library of Congress Cataloging-in-Publication Data

Names: Davis, Raymie, author.
Title: Family / Raymie Davis.
Description: Buffalo, NY : PowerKids Press, [2025] | Series: Let's learn American Sign Language
Identifiers: LCCN 2023036941 (print) | LCCN 2023036942 (ebook) | ISBN 9781499443486 (library binding) | ISBN 9781499443479 (paperback) | ISBN 9781499443493 (ebook)
Subjects: LCSH: American Sign Language--Juvenile literature. | Families--Juvenile literature.
Classification: LCC HV2476.4 .D37 2025 (print) | LCC HV2476.4 (ebook) | DDC 419/.7--dc23/eng/20230906
LC record available at https://lccn.loc.gov/2023036941
LC ebook record available at https://lccn.loc.gov/2023036942
Manufactured in the United States of America

CPSIA Compliance Information: Batch #CSPK25. For further information contact Rosen Publishing at 1-800-237-9932.